MW00626552

Impact 360

INSTITUTE

did Jesus rise from the dead?

WILLIAM LANE CRAIG, Ph.D.

Impact 360
INSTITUTE

Published in Pine Mountain, Georgia,
by Impact 360 Institute
(www.impact360institute.org).
Know. Be. Live.

Impact 360 Institute titles may be purchased in bulk
for educational, business, fund-raising, or sales promotional use.
For information, please e-mail info@impact360institute.org.

Editorial team: Jonathan Morrow, Miriam Drennan
Cover design: Ellen Parker Bibb

Softcover ISBN: 978-0-9915977-0-3
E-book ISBN: 978-0-9915977-1-0

Printed in the United States of America

Impact 360
INSTITUTE

We exist to equip a new generation of Christ-centered influencers to understand, defend, and live out their faith in the marketplace. Here are some of the ways we do this:

- **Immersion**—a 2-week Christian worldview and leadership training experience for high school students. (3 hours of college credit available)
- **Gap Year**—a 9-month academic experience that includes a month-long international mission trip to Brazil (18 hours of college credit)
- **Masters**—a unique and innovative graduate experience for young adults preparing to enter areas of higher education, student life, student campus ministry, or further graduate study.
- **Speakers Series**—Sign-up to be a part of Impact 360 Institute's Speaker Series LiveStream and be equipped to engage some of our culture's toughest questions.

FIND OUT MORE:

impact360institute.org

COMING SUMMER 2014!

"A robust natural theology may well be necessary for the gospel to be effectively heard in Western society today."

–DR. WILLIAM LANE CRAIG

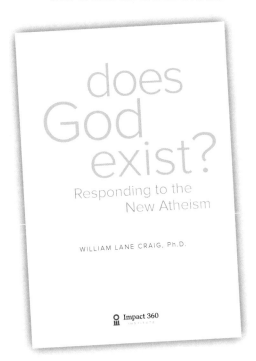

does
God
exist?
Responding to the
New Atheism

WILLIAM LANE CRAIG, Ph.D.

Impact 360

In his follow-up to *Did Jesus Rise from the Dead?*, Dr. Craig takes a departure from divine revelation to present the powerful philosophical, scientific, moral, and ontological arguments found in natural theology. Premise-by-premise, point-by-point, Dr. Craig qualifies and quantifies the case for God in language our post-Christian culture understands.

FIND OUT MORE:

impact360institute.org

Contents

INTRODUCTION

The Christian faith is predicated upon the remarkable claim that a historical person, Jesus of Nazareth, rose from the dead and therefore was, as he claimed, God's Son in a unique sense. But how credible is the claim of Jesus' resurrection? We will investigate that question historically.

Now one doesn't come to a study of Jesus' resurrection in a vacuum. Every investigator brings with him certain assumptions, which he presupposes in his inquiry and which, if challenged, might themselves become the subject of investigation and justification. Permit me, then, to state very clearly two presuppositions with which I approach our question.

First, I presuppose the existence of God, as demonstrated by the arguments of natural theology, such as the cosmological, teleological, and axiological arguments. This is the approach taken by classical defenders of the historicity of Jesus' resurrection such as Hugo Grotius, Samuel Clarke, and William Paley, as well as by such contemporary scholars as Wolfhart Pannenberg, Richard Swinburne, and Stephen Davis.

Now I realize that many people today don't share this presupposition; atheists and agnostics don't acknowledge the existence of a transcendent Creator and Designer of the universe. This is a huge difference in one's worldview that will, of course, radically affect how one assesses competing explanations of the facts. But our space and topic are limited, so if one is interested in the justification for belief in God's existence, one may consult my forthcoming book in this same series on that subject.[1]

Second, I presuppose that our background knowledge includes a good deal of information about the historical Jesus, including his radical personal claims, his teaching, and his crucifixion. In so doing, I stand squarely in the mainstream of New Testament scholarship concerning the historical Jesus. Again, I realize that radical critics don't share this presupposition. But the majority of New Testament scholars today agree that the historical Jesus possessed an unparalleled sense of authority, the authority to stand and speak in the place of God Himself. He claimed that in himself the Kingdom of God had come, and he carried out a ministry of miracle-working and exorcisms as signs of that fact. According to the German theologian Horst George Pöhlmann:

> *Today there is virtually a consensus . . . that Jesus came on the scene with an unheard of authority, with the claim of the authority to stand in God's place and speak to us and bring us to salvation. With regard to Jesus there are only two possible modes of behavior: either to believe that in him God encounters us or to nail him to the cross as a blasphemer.* Tertium non datur. *[There is no third way.]*[2]

So I'm also very safely situated with respect to my second presupposition.

An investigation of the historicity of the resurrection of Jesus will involve two steps: *First*, one must establish what facts are to be explained and, *second*, one must ask whether Jesus' resurrection is the best explanation of those facts. There are basically three main purported facts at issue:

1. the discovery of Jesus' empty tomb by a group of his female followers on the Sunday morning after his crucifixion;

2. various individuals and groups' experiencing appearances of Jesus alive after his death; and

3. the origin of the earliest disciples' belief that God had raised Jesus from the dead.

If these three facts can be established as historical, the question will then be whether they are best explained by what I'll call the "Resurrection Hypothesis"—namely, that God raised Jesus from the dead, or by some other explanation.

WHEN PROVING OR DISPROVING THE RESURRECTION, THREE FACTS MUST BE ADDRESSED:

• *The empty tomb*

• *The post-mortem appearances*

• *The origin of the Christian faith*

All historians recognize that Jesus of Nazareth met his untimely death by Roman crucifixion at the time of the Jewish Passover feast in Jerusalem. We therefore take that historical fact as given. The question then facing the historian is, What happened following Jesus' crucifixion? This book looks first at the facts to be explained, and then at competing explanations of these facts.

Part I:

THE EMPTY TOMB

There are at least five independent lines of evidence supporting the fact that the tomb in which Jesus was interred Friday evening after his crucifixion was found empty by a group of women on the following Sunday.

CHAPTER ONE

THE HISTORICAL CREDIBILITY

The historical credibility of Jesus' burial supports the historicity of the empty tomb. If the accounts of Jesus' burial in the Gospels are basically accurate, even given some divergence in the secondary details, then the location of Jesus' tomb was known in Jerusalem to both Jew and Christian alike. For according to the accounts, Jesus was buried by a member of the Jewish Sanhedrin named Joseph of Arimathea, and women who followed Jesus observed his burial. But in that case, the tomb must have been empty when the disciples began to preach that Jesus had risen from the dead.

> The tomb must have been empty when the disciples began to preach that Jesus had risen from the dead.

Three reasons underlie this inference:

- The disciples of Jesus could not have believed that Jesus had risen if his corpse still lay in the tomb. It would have been completely un-Jewish, not to say preposterous, to believe that a man whose dead body was known to lie in his tomb had been raised from the dead.

- Even if the disciples had been so rash as to proclaim Jesus' resurrection despite his occupied tomb, hardly anyone else would have believed them. One of the most noteworthy facts about the early Christian belief in Jesus' resurrection was that it flourished in the very city where Jesus had been publicly crucified. So long as the inhabitants of Jerusalem thought that Jesus' corpse lay in the tomb, few would have been prepared to believe such silliness as the claim that God had raised Jesus from the dead.

- Finally, even if people had believed that Jesus had risen, the Jewish authorities would have crushed the whole affair simply by pointing to Jesus' occupied tomb or perhaps even opening the tomb to reveal the corpse as decisive proof that Jesus had not risen back to life.

Even if the remains of the corpse were no longer recognizable due to putrefaction, the burden of proof would have still been upon anyone who said that these were *not* Jesus' remains. But no such dispute over the identification of Jesus' corpse ever seems to have taken place; the disputes between early Jewish non-Christians and Jewish Christians lay elsewhere, as we shall shortly see.

It won't do to suggest that the Jewish authorities didn't take the Christian movement seriously and so they didn't bother dealing with it. They were, after all, the same men who were responsible for Jesus' condemnation and delivery to the Romans for execution. As their engaging the Pharisee named Saul of Tarsus to persecute Jewish Christians amply illustrates, the Jewish authorities in Jerusalem were bent on squelching the budding Jesus movement.

Thus, if the story of Jesus' burial is historical in its core, then it is a very short inference to the fact that Jesus' tomb was also found to be vacant. For that reason, critics who deny the fact of the empty tomb have felt compelled to argue against the historicity of the burial as well. This is awkward, however, since the majority of New Testament critics today recognize Jesus' burial in the tomb by Joseph of Arimathea to be one of the best-established facts about the historical Jesus. While many a lengthy discussion could be had regarding the evidence for Jesus' burial, two points will suffice.

> Critics who deny the fact of the empty tomb have felt compelled to argue against the historicity of the burial as well.

First Point: Early, Eyewitness Accounts

First, *Jesus' burial is reported in extremely early, independent sources.* The Gospel of Mark is the earliest of the four Gospels, generally thought to have been written before AD 70. Most scholars think, however, that Mark used an even earlier source when writing his account of Jesus' suffering and death (the so-called the Passion Story), which most critics think is based on eyewitness testimony. The account of Jesus' burial in a tomb by Joseph of Arimathea is part of this pre-Markan, Passion source. Thus, we have here a very early source for Jesus' interment by Joseph.

Moreover, Paul in his first letter to the church in Corinth cites an old Christian tradition that he had received from the earliest disciples (1 Cor. 15:3–5). Paul probably received this tradition no later than his visit to Jerusalem in AD 36 after his conversion in AD 33 (Gal. 1:18), if not earlier while he was living in Damascus. This tradition, therefore, goes back to within the first five years after Jesus' crucifixion in AD 30. The tradition is a summary of the central points of early Christian proclamation. Its parallel form would have made it easy to memorize, and it may well have been used in Christian instruction. It runs:

- that Christ died for our sins in accordance with the Scriptures;
- and that he was buried;
- and that he was raised on the third day in accordance with the Scriptures;
- and that he appeared to Cephas, then to the Twelve.

Notice that the second line of this tradition refers to Jesus' burial. So, was the burial mentioned in Paul's tradition the same event as the burial by Joseph of Arimathea? We can answer that question by a comparison of Paul's four-line tradition with the Gospel narratives on the one hand and the sermons in the Acts of the Apostles.

ACCORDING TO PAUL . . . 1 CORINTHIANS 15:3−5	ACCORDING TO MARK . . . MARK 15:37−16:7	ACCORDING TO THE APOSTLES . . . ACTS 13:28−31
Christ died . . .	*Jesus uttered a loud cry and breathed his last.*	*They could charge him with nothing deserving death, yet they asked Pilate to have him killed.*
He was buried . . .	*Joseph bought a linen shroud, took him down, wrapped him in the shroud, and laid him in a tomb.*	*They took him down from the tree and laid him in a tomb.*
He was raised . . .	*". . . He has risen; he is not here. See the place where they laid him."*	*God raised him from the dead.*
He appeared . . .	*"But go, tell his disciples and Peter that he is going before you to Galilee. There you will see him, just as he told you."*	*For many days he appeared to those who traveled with him from Galilee to Jerusalem, who are now his witnesses to the people.*

This remarkable correspondence of independent traditions is convincing evidence that Paul's four-line tradition summarizes the basic events of Jesus' passion and resurrection, including his burial in the tomb. In the pre-Markan passion source and the pre-Pauline tradition delivered to the Corinthians, we thus have evidence from some of the earliest, independent sources in the New Testament for the burial of Jesus in the tomb.

And there are more; further independent testimonies to Jesus' burial by Joseph are also found in the sources behind the Gospels of Matthew, Luke, and John. Although the majority of scholars agree that Matthew and Luke used Mark's Gospel as one of their sources, the differences between Mark's account of the burial and those of Matthew and Luke suggest that they also had other sources than just Mark. Moreover, since scholars generally agree that the Gospel of John was written independently of the other three Gospels, we have yet another independent source for the burial in John's account. Finally, there are the early sermons in the Acts of the Apostles, which probably preserve the early preaching of the apostles. These sermons also refer to Jesus' interment in a tomb. Thus, we have the extraordinary number of at least five independent sources for Jesus' burial, some of which are extremely early.

Second Point: Joseph of Arimathea

The Gospels describe Joseph as a rich man, a member of the Jewish Sanhedrin. As a member of the Jewish Sanhedrin that condemned Jesus, Joseph of Arimathea is unlikely to be a Christian invention.

The Sanhedrin was a sort of Jewish high court made up of seventy of the leading men of Judaism, which presided in Jerusalem. There was an understandable hostility among early Christians toward the Jewish Sanhedrists, for Christians blamed the Sanhedrists for engineering a judicial murder of Jesus at the hands of the

Romans. The apostolic sermons in Acts, for example, go so far as to say that it was the Jewish leaders who crucified Jesus (Acts 2.23, 36; 4:10)!

> Jesus' burial by Joseph is very probably historical, since it would be almost inexplicable why Christians would invent a story about a Jewish Sanhedrist who gives Jesus a proper burial.

Therefore, Jesus' burial by Joseph is very probably historical, since it would be almost inexplicable why Christians would invent a story about a Jewish Sanhedrist who gives Jesus a proper burial.

For these and other reasons, the wide majority of New Testament scholars concur that after his crucifixion, Jesus was buried in a tomb by Joseph of Arimathea. According to the late John A. T. Robinson of Cambridge University, the burial of Jesus in the tomb is "one of the earliest and best-attested facts about Jesus."[3] But if Jesus' body was thus interred, then, as explained, it is very difficult to deny the fact that the tomb was later found empty.

CHAPTER TWO

INDEPENDENT ACCOUNTS

The discovery of Jesus' empty tomb is independently reported in very early sources. Mark's passion source probably did not end with the story of Jesus' burial, but with the story of the women's discovery of Jesus' empty tomb. For the burial story and the empty tomb story are really one story, forming a smooth, continuous narrative. They are united by grammatical and linguistic connections. Furthermore, it seems unlikely that the early Christians would have told a story of Jesus' passion, which just ended with his death and burial; the passion story is incomplete without the victory of the resurrection at the end. So Mark's passion source probably included and may have ended with the account of the women's discovery of the empty tomb.

> It seems unlikely that the early Christians would have told a story of Jesus' passion, which just ended with his death and burial; the passion story is incomplete without the victory of the resurrection at the end.

We've also seen that in 1 Corinthians 15:3–5 Paul cites an extremely early tradition that refers to Christ's burial and resurrection. Although the tradition does not explicitly mention the empty tomb, our earlier comparison of the four-line formula with the Gospel narratives and the sermons in Acts reveals that the third line of the tradition is, in fact, a summary of the story of the discovery of the empty tomb. Moreover, the empty tomb is implicit in two further features of Paul's tradition.

> In the minds of **first-century Jews**, there would have been **no question** that Jesus' tomb would have been empty as a result of his being raised.

First, the expression "he was raised" following the expression "he was buried" implies an empty tomb. The idea that someone could be buried and then raised from the dead and yet his body still remains in the grave is a peculiarity of modern theology! In the minds of first-century Jews, there would have been no question that Jesus' tomb would have been empty as a result of his being raised. Therefore, when the tradition states that Christ "was buried and he was raised," it automatically implies that an empty tomb was left behind.

Second, the expression "on the third day" implies the empty tomb. Since no one actually saw Jesus get up and walk out of the tomb, we must ask why the early disciples proclaimed that he had been raised "on the third day"? Why not the seventh day? The most likely answer is that it was on the third day after his crucifixion that the women discovered the tomb of Jesus empty; and so naturally, the resurrection itself came to be dated on that day.

We have, then, extremely early, independent evidence for the fact of Jesus' empty tomb in the pre-Markan and pre-Pauline material. The discovery of Jesus' empty tomb cannot therefore be written off as a later legendary development.

But there are other independent sources that account for the empty tomb, found in the other Gospels and Acts. Matthew is clearly working with an independent source, for he includes the story of the guard at the tomb, which is not derived from Mark and is unique to his Gospel; moreover, his comment that the rumor that the disciples had stolen Jesus' body, "And this story has been spread among the Jews to this day," (Matt. 28:15) shows that the guard is not Matthew's own creation, but was part of prior tradition. Luke also has an independent source, for he tells the story, not found in Mark, of two disciples' inspecting the tomb to verify the women's report that the tomb was vacant. This story cannot be regarded as Luke's own creation, since the incident is independently reported in John's Gospel. And, again, given John's independence of the other three Gospels, we have yet another independent report of the empty tomb.

Finally, in the sermons in the book of Acts, we have indirect references to Jesus' empty tomb. For example, Peter contrasts the tomb of King David with Jesus' tomb, saying, "the patriarch David that he both died and was buried, and his tomb is with us to this day," but "[Jesus], whom God raised up" (Acts 2:29-32; compare 13:36–37).

Historians consider they've hit historical pay dirt when they have two independent accounts of the same event. But in this case—the discovery of the empty tomb—we have no less than six independent sources, some of which are among the earliest materials to be found in the New Testament.

CHAPTER THREE

MARK'S ACCOUNT AND THE EMBARRASSMENT OF WOMEN WITNESSES

M ark's empty tomb story is simple and lacks signs of legendary development. His account of the women's discovery of the empty tomb is remarkably reserved and unembellished by theological motifs that would likely characterize a later legendary story.

For example, it is really quite amazing that the resurrection itself is not actually described or even witnessed, and there is no theological reflection on Jesus' conquering sin and death, no use of divine titles for Christ, no quotation of fulfilled prophecy, no description of the Risen Lord. Mark's narrative is very different than what one might expect from a Christian legend—just contrast Mark's account with the way in which Jesus' resurrection is vividly portrayed in modern passion plays!

To appreciate how restrained Mark's narrative is, we need only read the account in the second-century apocryphal Gospel of Peter. It describes Jesus' triumphant exit from the tomb as a gigantic figure whose head reaches above the clouds, supported by giant angels, followed by a talking cross, heralded by a voice from heaven, and all witnessed by a Roman guard, the Jewish leaders, and a multitude of spectators! This is how real legends look: They're richly decorated with theological and apologetical motifs. By contrast, Mark's account is stark in its simplicity.

And then, the Women Witnesses

The tomb was discovered empty by a group of Jesus' female followers. In order to appreciate this point, we need to understand two things about the place of women in first-century Jewish society.

First, women were not regarded as credible witnesses. The negative attitude toward the testimony of women is evident in the Jewish historian Josephus' description of Jewish rules for admissible testimony: "Let not the testimony of women be admitted, on account of the levity and boldness of their sex."[4] No such regulation is to be found in the Hebrew Scriptures; it is rather a reflection of the patriarchal society of first-century Judaism. It is noteworthy that the only times Josephus cites female witnesses in his histories is after the battles of Gamala and Masada when he is forced to recur to women for the simple reason that they were the only survivors of these slaughters.

Second, women occupied a low rung on the Jewish social ladder. Compared to men, women were, frankly, second-class citizens. The rabbis said: "Sooner let the words of the Law be burnt than delivered to women!"[5] and again: "Happy is he whose children are male, but unhappy is he whose children are female!"[6] The daily prayer of every Jewish man included the blessing, "Blessed are you, Lord our God, ruler of the universe, who has not created me a Gentile, a slave, or a woman."[7]

> If the empty tomb story were a legend, then male disciples would have been made to be the ones who discover the empty tomb.

Given their lower social status and lack of credibility as witnesses, it is quite amazing that it is *women* who are the discoverers of and principal witnesses to the fact of the empty tomb! If the empty tomb story were a legend, then male disciples would have been made to be the ones who discover the empty tomb. The fact that women—whose testimonies were deemed worthless—*were* the chief witnesses to the fact of the empty tomb can only be plausibly explained if, like it or not, they actually were the discoverers of the empty tomb, and the Gospel writers faithfully record what (for them) was an awkward and embarrassing fact.

CHAPTER FOUR

THE JEWISH POLEMIC

I f you think about it, the earliest Jewish polemic presupposes the fact of the empty tomb. As an example, see Matthew's attempt to refute the earliest Jewish response to the Christian proclamation of the resurrection:

The earliest Jewish polemic presupposes the fact of the empty tomb.

While they were going, behold, some of the guard went into the city and told the chief priests all that had taken place. And when they had assembled with the elders and taken counsel, they gave a sufficient sum of money to the soldiers and said, "Tell people, 'His disciples came by night and stole him away while we were asleep.' And if this comes to the governor's ears, we will satisfy him and keep you out of trouble." So they took the money and did as they were directed. And this story has been spread among the Jews to this day. –Matthew 28:11–15

Now our interest is not in the historicity of Matthew's story of the guard at the tomb but rather in his incidental remark at the story's close: "This story has been spread among the Jews to this day." This remark reveals that Matthew was concerned about refuting a widespread Jewish explanation of the resurrection.

So what were unbelieving Jews saying in response to the disciples' proclamation "He is risen from the dead"? That these men were full of new wine? That Jesus' corpse still lay in the tomb? No. They were saying, "His disciples came by night and stole him away."

Think about that: "His disciples came by night and stole him away." The Jewish authorities did not deny the fact that Jesus' tomb was empty; instead they entangled themselves in a hopeless series of absurdities, trying to explain it away. In other words, the Jewish claim that the disciples stole the body presupposes that the body was, in fact, missing. Therefore, we have evidence from the very adversaries of the early Christian movement for the fact of the empty tomb.

> We have evidence from the very adversaries of the early Christian movement for the fact of the empty tomb.

These five lines of evidence, taken together, give sufficient grounds for thinking that Jesus' tomb was, in fact, found empty on the first day of the week by a group of his female followers. Most scholars, therefore, regard the fact of Jesus' empty tomb to be well-established. According to Jacob Kremer, a New Testament critic who has specialized in the study of the resurrection: "By far most exegetes hold firmly to the reliability of the biblical statements about the empty tomb."[8] In fact, in a survey of over two thousand publications on the resurrection in English, French, and German since 1975, Gary Habermas found that seventy-five percent of scholars who have written on the subject accept the historicity of the women's discovery of Jesus' empty tomb.[9] The evidence has convinced even a number of Jewish scholars, such as Pinchas Lapide and Geza Vermes, that Jesus' tomb was found empty. Therefore, we can regard the first of the three facts to be explained as, if not beyond dispute, historically well-established.

Part II:

POST-MORTEM APPEARANCES

Did people really see Jesus alive after his death? We will begin our inquiry by first considering the evidence for the resurrection appearances of Jesus: there are three main lines of evidence that bear examination.

Paul's list of eyewitnesses, cited in 1 Corinthians 15:3–8, to Jesus' resurrection appearances substantiates the occurrence of such appearances. Let's look briefly at each appearance in Paul's list to see whether it's plausible that such an event actually occurred.

CHAPTER FIVE

PETER, THE DISCIPLES, AND THE FIVE HUNDRED

For I delivered to you as of first importance what I also received: that Christ died for our sins in accordance with the Scriptures, that he was buried, that he was raised on the third day in accordance with the Scriptures, and that he appeared to Cephas, then to the twelve. Then he appeared to more than five hundred brothers at one time, most of whom are still alive, though some have fallen asleep. Then he appeared to James, then to all the apostles. Last of all, as to one untimely born, he appeared also to me. —1 Corinthians 15:3–8

T he Gospels do not contain the story of Christ appearing to Peter (or "Cephas," as Paul writes in the Aramaic). But it was included in the old Christian tradition passed on by Paul, which came out of the Jerusalem church. Moreover, Paul himself vouches for it. We know from Paul's letter to the Galatians 1:18 that three years after his conversion on the Damascus Road, Paul spent about two weeks with Peter in Jerusalem. So Paul knew whether or not Peter claimed to have had such an experience. Moreover, the appearance to Peter is independently mentioned in another old Christian tradition found in Luke 24:34: "The Lord has risen indeed, and has appeared to Simon!" That Luke is passing on a prior tradition and not just composing freehand here is evident from the awkward way in which this saying is inserted into his story of the appearance to the Emmaus

> Virtually all New Testament scholars agree that, however you might care to explain it, Peter did see a post-mortem appearance of Jesus.

disciples. So we have multiple, independent, and extremely early sources for the fact of this appearance to Peter. Therefore, virtually all New Testament scholars agree that, however you might care to explain it, Peter did see a post-mortem appearance of Jesus.

The Disciples

The next appearance mentioned was to "the twelve," undoubtedly the original group of twelve disciples who had been chosen by Jesus during his ministry—minus, of course, Judas, whose absence didn't affect the formal title of the group. This is the best-attested resurrection appearance of Jesus. It is also a part of that very early tradition that Paul hands on. Moreover, Paul himself had personal contact with members of The Twelve. In addition we actually have two independent accounts of this appearance in Luke 24:36–42 and John 20:19–20. There can be little doubt that such an appearance occurred, for it is attested in the old Christian tradition, vouched for by Paul, and independently described by both Luke and John.

The Five Hundred

For whatever reason, the five hundred witnesses (and others he mentions beyond that) were not, apparently, part of the traditional formula he was using, but who were known to him nonetheless.

The number of people involved—five hundred, simultaneously—

is noteworthy, and yet there is no mention whatsoever of this appearance anywhere else in the New Testament. One may be pardoned for being somewhat skeptical that so extraordinary an event, should it have occurred, could have gone unnoticed by the biblical authors, but Paul himself seems to have had personal contact with these individuals, since he knew that some had died in the meantime.

> The number of people involved—five hundred, simultaneously—is noteworthy, and yet there is no mention whatsoever of this appearance anywhere else in the New Testament.

He notes this in his passing comment, "most of whom are still alive, though some have fallen asleep." Why does Paul add this remark? The great New Testament scholar of Cambridge University, C. H. Dodd, replies, "There can hardly be any purpose in mentioning the fact that the most of the 500 are still alive, unless Paul is saying, in effect, 'The witnesses are there to be questioned.'"[10] Paul would not have said this if the event had not occurred. He wouldn't have challenged people to talk to the eyewitnesses if the event had never taken place and there were no eyewitnesses. But evidently there were witnesses to this event, and Paul knew that some of them had died in the interim. Therefore, the event must have taken place.

Perhaps this appearance is not related in the Gospels because it took place in Galilee. As one traces the various appearances narrated in the Gospels, it seems that they occurred first in Jerusalem, then in Galilee, and then back in Jerusalem again. An appearance to five hundred people would

> It was in Galilee that thousands had flocked to hear Jesus teach.

have to have occurred outdoors, perhaps on a hillside near a Galilean village. Recall that it was in Galilee that thousands had flocked to hear Jesus teach. Since the Gospels focus on the appearances that occurred in Jerusalem rather than in Galilee, none of them narrates the story of the appearance to the five hundred. An intriguing possibility, however, is that the appearance to the five hundred was the appearance in Galilee predicted by the angel at the tomb and then described by Matthew (28.16–17).

CHAPTER SIX

JAMES AND THE OTHER APOSTLES, INCLUDING SAUL OF TARSUS

J esus' post-mortem to his younger brother James is perhaps one of the most amazing of all, for it was apparent that neither James nor any of Jesus' younger brothers believed in Jesus during his lifetime (Mark 3:21, 31–35; John 7:1–10). They didn't believe he was the Messiah, or a prophet, or even anybody special. By the criterion of embarrassment, the unbelief of Jesus' own family is undoubtedly a historical fact.

After the resurrection, however, we're surprised to find Jesus' brothers among the Christian believers gathered in the upper room in Jerusalem (Acts 1:14). They are not mentioned again until the story of Peter's deliverance from prison by the angel (Acts 12:17). Peter's first words after his escape are, "Report this to James." In his letter to the churches of Galatia, Paul tells of his two-week visit to Jerusalem about three years after his experience on the Damascus Road. He says that apart from Peter, he saw none of the other apostles except James, the Lord's brother (Gal. 1:19). Paul at least implies that James was now considered to be one of the apostles. Paul tells us that when he visited Jerusalem again fourteen years later, he conferred with the three "pillars" of the church in Jerusalem: Peter, John, and James (Galatians 2:9). Finally, we find that in Acts 21:18, James is the sole head of the Jerusalem church and of the council of elders. There is no information about James' later life in the New Testament; but from Josephus, the Jewish historian, we discover that sometime after AD 60 the Sanhedrin stoned James to death illegally for his faith in Christ.[11]

Jesus' other brothers became believers as well, and were active in Christian preaching, as we see from Paul's comment in 1 Corinthians 9:5: "Do we not have the right to take along a believing wife, as do the other apostles and the brothers of the Lord and Cephas?"

Now, how does one explain this? On one hand, it seems certain that Jesus' brothers did not believe in him during his lifetime; on the other, it's equally certain that they became ardent Christians who were active in ministry. Jesus' crucifixion would not account for this transformation, since Jesus' execution would only confirm in James' mind that his brother's Messianic pretensions were delusory, just as he had thought.

> What would it take to make you believe that your brother is the Lord, so that you would die for this belief, as James did?

Most of us have brothers. What would it take to make you believe that your brother is the Lord, so that you would die for this belief, as James did? Can there be any doubt that the reason for this amazing transformation is the fact that "then he appeared to James"? Even the skeptical New Testament critic Hans Grass acknowledges that James' conversion is one of the surest proofs of the resurrection of Jesus Christ.[12]

ACCORDING TO 1 CORINTHIANS 15:3–8,
THE RESURRECTED CHRIST APPEARED TO:

Peter	*James (Jesus' biological brother)*
The Twelve (minus Judas)	*All Other Apostles*
500 Witnesses, simultaneously	*Saul of Tarsus*

The Other Apostles

The next appearance Paul notes is to "all the apostles." We can't be sure who this vaguely characterized group was, but more than likely it was limited to a limited circle of Christian missionaries that was somewhat wider than the Twelve. The existence of such a group is attested in Acts 1:21–22. The historicity of this appearance is guaranteed by Paul's personal contact with the apostles themselves.

Saul of Tarsus

The final appearance mentioned by Paul is just as amazing as the appearance to James: "last of all," he writes, "he appeared also to me." Luke tells the story of Jesus' appearance to Saul of Tarsus (a.k.a., Paul) just outside Damascus in Acts 9:1–9 and repeats it twice. That this event actually occurred is established beyond doubt by Paul's references to it in his own letters.

The incident on the Damascus Road changed Saul's whole life. He was a rabbi, a Pharisee, a respected Jewish leader. He hated the Christian heresy and did everything he could to stamp it out. He says in his letters that he was even responsible for the execution of Christian believers! Then suddenly, he gave up everything—including his position as a respected Jewish leader—and became a Christian missionary. He entered a

> Paul gave up everything—including his position as a respected Jewish leader—and became a Christian missionary.

life of poverty, labor, and suffering. He was whipped, beaten, and stoned; left for dead; shipwrecked three times; and remained in constant danger, deprivation, and anxiety. Finally, he made the ultimate sacrifice and was martyred for his faith at Rome. And it was all because on that day outside Damascus, he saw "Jesus our Lord" (l Cor. 9:1).

> *Am I not free? Am I not an apostle? Have I not seen Jesus our Lord? Are not you my workmanship in the Lord?*
> −1 Corinthians 9:1

To summarize, Paul's testimony establishes historically that various individuals and groups of people on different occasions experienced appearances of Jesus alive after his death.

CHAPTER SEVEN

CONCLUSIONS

The Gospel accounts provide multiple, independent accounts of post-mortem appearances of Jesus, even some of the same people mentioned in Paul's list. There are several conclusions to be drawn from these sources, which are also supported by other sources not found in the canon.

The appearance to Peter is independently attested by Paul and Luke (1 Cor. 15.5; Luke 24:34) and is universally acknowledged by critics to be historical. The appearance to the Twelve is independently attested by Paul, Luke, and John (1 Cor. 15.5; Luke 24:36–43; John 20:19–20) and is also undisputed by historical scholars. The appearance to the women is independently attested by Matthew and John (Matt. 28:9–10; John 20:11–17) and also enjoys ratification by the criterion of embarrassment, given the low credibility accorded a woman's testimony at that time. Most scholars think that the reason this appearance is not included in the list of witnesses quoted by Paul is the futility of citing female witnesses. And finally, Mark, Matthew, and John independently attest to Jesus' appearance to the disciples in Galilee. (Mark 16:7; Matt. 28:16–17; John 21)

The appearances take place in Jerusalem, then Galilee, and then Jerusalem again, matching the pilgrimages of the disciples as they returned to Galilee following the Passover/Feast of Unleavened

Bread in Jerusalem and then traveled again to Jerusalem two months later for Pentecost.

> We can explain these post-mortem appearances as hallucinations if we want to, but what **we cannot** do responsibly is deny that they ever occurred.

So, what should we conclude from this evidence? We can explain these appearances as hallucinations if we want to, but what we cannot do responsibly is deny that they ever occurred. Even the skeptical German critic Gerd Lüdemann is emphatic: "It may be taken as historically certain that Peter and the disciples had experiences after Jesus' death in which Jesus appeared to them as the risen Christ."[13] The evidence firmly establishes that on separate occasions, different individuals and groups had experiences of seeing Jesus alive from the dead. Scarcely any historical scholar today disputes this conclusion.

We can also conclude that the Resurrected Christ's appearances were physical, bodily appearances. The evidence I've presented thus far leaves it open whether the resurrection appearances were physical or merely visionary in nature; we'll examine later whether even visionary experiences of the risen Jesus can be plausibly explained on purely psychological grounds. But if the appearances were physical and bodily in nature, then a purely psychological explanation becomes virtually impossible—so it's worth asking, What we can know about the nature of the resurrection appearances?

So is it with the resurrection of the dead. What is sown is perishable; what is raised is imperishable. It is sown in dishonor; it is raised in glory. It is sown in weakness; it is raised in power. It is sown a natural body; it is raised a spiritual body. If there is a natural body, there is also a spiritual body. —1 Corinthians 15:42–44

Paul implies that the appearances were physical in two ways. He conceives of the resurrection body as physical; all commentators recognize that Paul does not teach the immortality of the soul alone, but rather the resurrection of the body. In 1 Corinthians 15:42–44, Paul draws four essential contrasts between the present, earthly body and our future, resurrection body.

THE EARTHLY BODY IS:	BUT THE RESURRECTION BODY IS:
mortal	*immortal*
dishonorable	*glorious*
weak	*powerful*
natural	*spiritual*

Only the last of these contrasts might lead us to believe that Paul didn't believe in a physical, resurrection body. But we must ask what Paul meant by the words, which I've translated as "natural/spiritual"?

The Greek word for *natural*, when translated, literally means "soul-ish." Now it's evident that Paul doesn't mean that our earthly bodies are made out of soul. Rather, his use of "natural" means "dominated by, or pertaining to, human nature."

By the same token, when he says our resurrection bodies will be "spiritual," he doesn't mean that they will be made out of spirit. Rather, he means "dominated by, or oriented toward, the Spirit." It's the same sense of "spiritual" as when we say that someone is a spiritual person.

We can be sure of Paul's meaning by looking at the way Paul uses precisely these same words in 1 Corinthians 2:14–15, several chapters earlier and within the same letter.

> *The natural person does not accept the things of the Spirit of God, for they are folly to him, and he is not able to understand them because they are spiritually discerned. The spiritual person judges all things, but is himself to be judged by no one.* −1 Corinthians 2:14–15

Clearly *natural person* doesn't mean physical person; rather, a person oriented toward human nature. Similarly, *spiritual person* doesn't mean an intangible, invisible person; it refers to a person oriented toward the Spirit. We find the same contrast in 1 Corinthians 15. The present, earthly body will be freed from its domination by sinful human nature and will become, instead, fully empowered and directed by God's Spirit. Paul's doctrine of the resurrection body therefore implies a physical resurrection.

The second way Paul, along with the rest of the New Testament, implies a physical resurrection is that he distinguishes a *resurrection appearance* of Jesus from a *vision* of Jesus. The resurrection appearances of Jesus soon ceased, but people continued to see visions of Jesus in glory. Now the question is: What is the difference between a resurrection appearance and a vision of Jesus?

The answer of the New Testament seems to be clear: A vision, even though caused by God, was purely in the mind of the visionary, whereas a resurrection appearance was an extra-mental event in the external world.

We can compare Stephen's vision of Jesus described in Acts 7 with the various resurrection appearances of Jesus. Stephen saw a vision of a man—not a man who was physically present, for no one else experienced anything at all—and it was a completely private experience. By contrast, the resurrection appearances were not inner, subjective experiences—they could be experienced by anybody who was there.

Paul had visions of Jesus in his life as a Christian; but he could properly regard his experience on the Damascus Road as a resurrection appearance of Jesus rather than a vision, even though it took place after Jesus' ascension, because it involved phenomena in the external world, such as the light and the voice, which Paul's traveling companions also experienced to varying degrees. Therefore, the distinction between a vision and a resurrection appearance of Jesus also implies that the resurrection appearances were physical.

> A vision, even though caused by God, was purely in the mind of the visionary, whereas a resurrection appearance was an extra-mental event in the external world.

Now, the Gospel-appearance narratives also show that the appearances were physical and bodily; in fact, every resurrection appearance cited in the Gospels unanimously testifies to a physical, bodily appearance. If you think about it, that's really impressive; had *none* of the original appearances been a physical, bodily appearance, then it would be very strange to have a completely unanimous testimony in the Gospels that *all* of them were physical, with no trace of the supposed original, visionary appearances. It's unlikely that such thorough corruption of oral tradition would occur in so short a time, especially while the original eyewitnesses were still about.

Now if all the appearances were originally non-physical visions, then we're at a complete loss to explain the rise of the Gospel appearance narratives. For physical, bodily appearances would be folly to Gentiles and a stumbling block to Jews—since neither could embrace the notion of physical resurrection of the dead—but both would have been quite happy to accept claims of visionary appearances of the deceased.

In all honesty, we have to say that the only basis for denying the physical, bodily nature of the post-mortem appearances of Jesus is not historical, but philosophical; namely, such appearances would be stupendous miracles, and many critics simply cannot swallow that claim. But if that's the problem, then we need to go back to square one and think about the question of God's existence; if God exists, there's no good reason to be skeptical about miracles. For as the agnostic philosopher Peter Slezak nicely put it in our debate on God's existence, for a God who is able to create the entire universe, the odd resurrection would be child's play! Unfortunately, most New Testament scholars are not trained in philosophy and therefore, make elementary blunders when it comes to these questions.

On the basis of the aforementioned evidence, we can conclude that the fact of Jesus' post-mortem appearances to various individuals and groups under a variety of circumstances is firmly established historically and, moreover, that these appearances were bodily and physical.

Part III

THE ORIGIN OF
THE CHRISTIAN FAITH

*Now we come to the third fact to be explained:
the very origin of the Christian faith. Everybody
knows that Christianity sprang into being midway
through the first century AD, but that raises the
obvious question: Why did it come into existence?
What caused this movement to begin? Even skeptical New Testament scholars recognize that the
Christian faith owes its origin to the earliest disciples' belief that God had raised Jesus from the dead.
In fact, they pinned nearly everything on this belief.*

CHAPTER EIGHT

CONVICTION OF THE PROMISED MESSIAH

J ews had no conception whatsoever of a Messiah who, instead of triumphing over Israel's enemies, would be shamefully executed by them as a criminal. *Messiah* was supposed to be a triumphant figure who would command the respect of Jew and Gentile alike, and who would establish the throne of David in Jerusalem. Yet Jesus' disciples held deeply a conviction that he was the promised Messiah—a Messiah who failed to deliver and to reign; was defeated, humiliated, and slain by his enemies; and was a contradiction in terms. Nowhere do ancient Jewish texts speak of this sort of "Messiah." So it's difficult to exaggerate, therefore, what a catastrophe Jesus' crucifixion would have been for the disciples. It wasn't just that their beloved teacher was gone; rather, Jesus' death on the cross meant the crushing defeat of any hopes they had entertained that he was the Messiah.

> Jesus' disciples held deeply a conviction that he was the promised Messiah—a Messiah who failed to deliver and to reign; was defeated, humiliated, and slain by his enemies; and was a contradiction in terms.

How is it, then, that the Jesus movement continued? The disciples suddenly and sincerely came to believe that God had raised Jesus from the dead. The resurrection of Jesus reversed the catastrophe of the crucifixion. Since God had raised Jesus from the dead, Jesus was seen to be Messiah after all.

Therefore, Peter proclaims in Acts 2:23, 36: "This Jesus, delivered up according to the definite plan and foreknowledge of God, you crucified and killed by the hands of lawless men. . . . Let all the house of Israel therefore know for certain that God has made him both Lord and Christ, this Jesus whom you crucified." It was on the basis of belief in his resurrection that the disciples could believe that Jesus was, indeed, the Messiah.

It's not surprising, then, that the belief in Jesus' resurrection was universal in the early church. The tradition that Paul cites in 1 Corinthians 15:3–7, which defines the Gospel as the death, burial, resurrection, and appearances of Christ, shows that this understanding of the Gospel goes all the way back to the very beginning of the church in Jerusalem.

The Belief of the Resurrection Itself

Thus, the origin of the Christian movement hinges on the belief of the earliest disciples that God had raised Jesus from the dead. But now the obvious question cannot be avoided: How do we explain the origin of *that* belief? As R. H. Fuller says, even the most skeptical critic must posit some mysterious X to get the movement going.[14] But the question is: What was that X?

> The origin of the Christian movement hinges on the belief of the earliest disciples that God had raised Jesus from the dead.

Summary

Before moving forward, let's review all three of our main points:

- First, we saw that numerous lines of historical evidence prove that the tomb of Jesus was found empty by a group of his women followers.

- Second, we saw that several lines of historical evidence establish that on numerous occasions and in different places various individuals and groups saw appearances of Jesus alive from the dead.

- And finally, third, we saw that the very origin of the Christian faith depends on the belief of the earliest disciples that God had raised Jesus of Nazareth from the dead.

> The only point of serious disagreement would be on the physical nature of the resurrection appearances.

These three great, independently established facts represent *the majority view* of New Testament critics today. The only point of serious disagreement would be on the physical nature of the resurrection appearances. But the state of current scholarship strongly supports the three facts as I have stated them. These are not merely the conclusions of conservative or evangelical scholars; these are the conclusions of mainstream, New Testament criticism. As we saw, three-quarters of scholars who have written on the subject accept the fact of the empty tomb; virtually no one today denies that the earliest disciples experienced post-mortem appearances of Jesus; and far and away, most scholars agree that the earliest disciples at least believed that God had raised Jesus from the dead. It's the critic who would deny these facts that today finds himself on the defensive.

CHAPTER NINE

THE INCONSISTENCIES

W e need not therefore worry about inconsistencies in the circumstantial details of the Gospel resurrection. The case for the historicity of Jesus' resurrection doesn't depend on such details. All four Gospels attest to the key, basic facts; many more details can be supplied by adding facts that are documented in three out of four.

> All four Gospels attest to the key, basic facts.

ALL FOUR GOSPELS AGREE THAT:

Jesus of Nazareth was crucified in Jerusalem by Roman authority during the Passover Feast.

Having been arrested and convicted on charges of blasphemy by the Jewish Sanhedrin, he was then slandered before the Roman prefect Pontius Pilate on charges of treason.

He died within several hours and was buried Friday afternoon by Joseph of Arimathea in a tomb, which was sealed with a stone.

Certain women followers of Jesus, including Mary Magdalene, having observed his interment, visited his tomb early on Sunday morning, only to find it empty.

Thereafter, Jesus appeared alive from the dead to the disciples, including Peter, who then became proclaimers of the message of his resurrection.

Minor discrepancies in the resurrection narratives don't affect our case here; in fact, historians expect to find inconsistencies even in the most reliable sources.

> Historians expect to find inconsistencies even in the most reliable sources.

No historian simply throws out a source because it has inconsistencies; otherwise, we'd have to be skeptical about all secular, historical narratives that also contain such inconsistencies. The result would be a wholly unreasonable historical skepticism.

Moreover, in the case of the Gospels, the inconsistencies aren't even within a single source; they're between independent sources. But obviously, it doesn't follow from an inconsistency between two independent sources that both sources are wrong; at worst, one is wrong if they can't be harmonized.

> The inconsistencies among the Gospel accounts aren't even within a single source; they're between independent sources.

The remaining issue, then, is how the three established facts I've stated are best explained.

Part IV

EXPLAINING THE EVIDENCE

We come at length to the second step in our case: determining which explanation of the evidence is the best.

CHAPTER TEN

ASSESSING HYPOTHESES

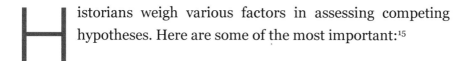

istorians weigh various factors in assessing competing hypotheses. Here are some of the most important:[15]

1. The best explanation has greater *explanatory scope* than other explanations. That is, it explains more of the evidence.

2. The best explanation has greater *explanatory power* than other explanations. That is, it makes the evidence more probable.

3. The best explanation is *more plausible* than other explanations. That is, it fits better with true background beliefs.

4. The best explanation is less *contrived* than other explanations. That is, it doesn't require adopting as many new beliefs for which we have no independent evidence.

5. The best explanation is *disconfirmed by fewer accepted beliefs* than other explanations. That is, it doesn't conflict with as many accepted beliefs.

6. The best explanation meets conditions 1–5 so much better than the others that there's little chance that one of the other explanations, after further investigation, will do better in meeting these conditions.

Since proposed hypotheses may do really well in meeting some of these criteria but not so well in meeting others, figuring out which hypothesis is the best explanation may often be difficult and requires skill. But if the explanatory scope and power of a hypothesis are very great, and it does a much better job in explaining a wide variety of facts, then it's likely to be the best explanation.

So now that we've covered how we assess, let's now apply these criteria to the typical hypotheses that have been offered down through history to explain the empty tomb, the post-mortem appearances, and the origin of the disciples' belief in Jesus' resurrection; using this standard of assessment, each hypothesis has the same opportunity to do better or as well in explaining these facts as the Resurrection Hypothesis that God raised Jesus from the dead.

CHAPTER ELEVEN

CONSPIRACY HYPOTHESIS

Accoding to the Conspiracy Hypothesis, the disciples stole Jesus' body out of the tomb and then lied to people about his appearances, so that Jesus' resurrection was a hoax. This was the very first counter-explanation for the empty tomb, mentioned in Matthew's Gospel, and European Deists revived it during the eighteenth century. Today, however, this hypothesis has been completely abandoned by modern scholarship. To see why, let's apply to it the standard criteria for testing historical hypotheses.

1. *Explanatory scope:* The Conspiracy Hypothesis does offer explanations of the full range of the evidence: It provides an explanation of the empty tomb (namely, the disciples stole Jesus' body); the post-mortem appearances (the disciples made these up); and the origin of the disciples' (supposed) belief in Jesus'

> According to the Conspiracy Hypothesis, the disciples stole Jesus' body out of the tomb and then lied to people about his appearances, so that Jesus' resurrection was a hoax.

resurrection (again, they made it up). The question is whether these explanations meet the remaining criteria.

2. *Explanatory power:* So what about the explanatory power of the Conspiracy Hypothesis? First, consider the fact of the empty tomb; if the disciples had stolen Jesus' body, then why would they make up a story about *women* discovering the tomb to be empty? That wouldn't be the sort of story Jewish men would invent. Moreover, the Conspiracy Hypothesis does a poor job of explaining the simplicity of the empty tomb story. Where are the Old Testament proof-texts, the fulfilled prophecies? Why is there no description of Jesus' resurrection, as we find in later forgeries like the Gospel of Peter? Moreover, the Conspiracy Hypothesis doesn't explain the argument between Christian Jews and non-Christian Jews very well; if the disciples just made up the story of the guard at the tomb, then why doesn't Mark's Gospel tell the story? Even in Matthew's story, the guard is set too late to preclude theft of the body: The disciples could have stolen it before the *guard* arrived on Saturday morning, so that they were actually guarding an empty tomb! To see how an invented story would look, see again the forged Gospel of Peter, where the guard is set immediately on Friday, when Jesus is buried.

The Conspiracy Hypothesis also has trouble explaining the evidence for the appearances. A Jewish person making up such stories would probably describe Jesus' resurrection appearances in terms of visions of God, and descriptions of the end-time resurrection in the Old Testament (as in Dan. 12:2). But then, wouldn't the stories describe Jesus' appearing to the disciples in dazzling glory? And why isn't the resurrection itself described? Why are there no made-up stories of appearances to the high priest Caiaphas or to the members the Sanhedrin, as Jesus predicted? Making up stories of how Jesus appeared to them would have the advantage that then they could be branded as the real liars, not the disciples, for denying that Jesus did appear to them!

But the Conspiracy Hypothesis is undoubtedly the weakest

when it comes to explaining the origin of the disciples' belief in Jesus' resurrection. For the hypothesis really *denies* that fact; instead, it seeks to explain only why it *appeared* that the disciples believed in Jesus' resurrection. But as scholars have universally recognized, you can't plausibly deny that the earliest disciples at least sincerely *believed* that God had raised Jesus from the dead with so much conviction that they were willing to die for that belief. The transformation in the lives of the disciples cannot be plausibly explained by saying that they were liars and hoaxers; this problem alone has served to sink the old Conspiracy Hypothesis forever.

3. *Plausibility:* It gets even worse when we come to the plausibility of the Conspiracy Hypothesis. Here we might mention objections to the unbelievable complexity of such a conspiracy or the unlikelihood of the disciples' being psychologically disposed to such a conspiracy; but the problem that dwarfs all others is that it's completely anachronistic to imagine that first century Jews would try to hoax Jesus' resurrection.

You see, the Conspiracy Hypothesis looks at the disciples in the rearview mirror of Christian history rather than from the perspective of a first-century Jew. In ancient Judaism, there was no conception of a Messiah who, instead of conquering Israel's enemies and re-establishing David's throne in Jerusalem, would be shamefully executed by his enemies as a criminal. Moreover, the idea of being raised from the dead was just unrelated to the idea of Messiah and even incompatible with it, since Messiah wasn't supposed to be killed! As the British New Testament historian N. T. Wright nicely puts it, if you're a first-century Jew, and your favorite Messiah got himself crucified, then you've basically got two choices: Either you go home, or get yourself a new Messiah. But the disciples would never have come up with the outlandish and un-Jewish idea of stealing Jesus' corpse and saying that God had raised him from the dead.

Many popularizers today suggest that early Christians could have come up with the idea of Jesus' resurrection through the influence of pagan mythology. Back around the turn of the twentieth century, scholars in comparative religion combed the literature of ancient mythology looking for parallels to Christian beliefs, and some even thought to explain Christian beliefs, like the belief in Jesus' resurrection, as the result of the influence of such myths. The movement soon collapsed, however, for two reasons: the myths were not really parallel and there was no causal connection.

Parallels

You see, the ancient world was a cornucopia of myths of various gods and heroes. Comparative studies in religion demand sensitivity on the part of the scholar to their similarities and differences; otherwise, the result is inevitable distortion and confusion.

Unfortunately, scholars eager to find parallels to Jesus' resurrection failed to exercise such sensitivity, so many of the supposed parallels are actually stories of the *assumption* of the hero into heaven (Hercules, Romulus). Others are *disappearance* stories, which claim that the hero has disappeared into a higher realm (Apollonius of Tyana, Empedocles). Still others are just *seasonal symbols* for the crop cycle, as the crops die in the dry season and come back to life in the rainy season (Tammuz, Osiris, Adonis). And finally, some are *political expressions* of emperor worship (Julius Caesar, Caesar Augustus).

None of these ideas is parallel to the Jewish idea of the resurrection of the dead. In fact, most scholars have come to doubt whether there really were *any* myths of dying and rising gods at all in the ancient near east. For example, in the myth of Osiris, which was one of the best-known symbolic seasonal myths, Osiris doesn't really come back to life—he just continues to exist in the realm of the dead.

Generally speaking, scholars have come to realize that pagan mythology is just the wrong interpretive framework in which to correctly understand Jesus of Nazareth. Jesus and his disciples were first-century Israelite Jews, and it's in that context that they must be understood. The spuriousness of the alleged parallels is one specific indication that pagan mythology is the wrong interpretive context for understanding the disciples' belief in Jesus' resurrection.

Causal Connections

So with that point in mind, there was no causal connection between the pagan myths and the disciples' belief in Jesus' resurrection. Jews were certainly familiar with the seasonal deities (Ezek. 37:1–14) . . . and found them abhorrent. For that reason, we don't find any trace of cults with dying and rising gods in first century Israel.

At any rate, it's highly unlikely that the Jesus' disciples would have come up with the idea that Jesus was risen from the dead because they had heard pagan myths about dying and rising seasonal gods. As a result, historical scholars have abandoned this approach. That such a hypothesis is still repeated endlessly today in popular literature is sad testimony to the chasm that exists between scholarly work on Jesus and pop culture.

So if the influence of pagan myths is not the source of the idea of Jesus' resurrection, what about Jewish influences? Jews already believed in the resurrection of the dead; perhaps the disciples came up with the idea of saying Jesus was risen as a result of the influence of Jewish beliefs about the afterlife?

Again, this is unlikely, for the Jewish doctrine of resurrection differed in at least two fundamental ways from Jesus' resurrection; to put it simply, it differed in the *when* and the *who.*

Jews believed that the resurrection to glory and immortality only took place after the end of the world; they had no concept of, much less belief in, a resurrection within history. It's no wonder, then, that the disciples were so confused by Jesus' predictions of his own resurrection—naturally, they thought he was talking about the resurrection at the end of the world. In Mark 9:9–11, for example, we're told:

> *And as they were coming down the mountain, he charged them to tell no one what they had seen, until the Son of Man had risen from the dead. So they kept the matter to themselves, questioning what this rising from the dead might mean. And they asked him, "Why do the scribes say that first Elijah must come?"*

Jesus predicts his resurrection, and what do the disciples ask? "Why is it that the scribes say that first Elijah must come?" Jews believed that the prophet Elijah would come again before the Day of the Lord, the judgment day on which the dead would be raised. The disciples had no idea of a resurrection occurring *prior* to the end of the world; therefore, Jesus' predictions of his own resurrection only confused them.

So given their Jewish mindset, the disciples after Jesus' crucifixion would not have come up with the idea that he had been already raised from the dead. They would have only looked forward

> The disciples had no idea of a resurrection occurring prior to the end of the world; therefore, Jesus' predictions of his own resurrection only confused them.

to the resurrection on the final judgment day and, in keeping with Jewish practices, perhaps kept his tomb as a shrine where his bones could rest until the resurrection.

Now Jews also believed that the resurrection was the resurrection of *all* the righteous dead—not the isolated resurrection of an individual. Moreover, there was no connection between the individual believer's resurrection and the prior resurrection of the Messiah, and, indeed, no belief in Messiah's prior resurrection at all. That's why we find no examples of other messianic movements claiming that their executed leader was risen from the dead. N. T. Wright has been emphatic about this point:

> All the followers of those first century messianic movements were fanatically committed to the cause . . . But in no case right across the century before Jesus and the century after him do we hear of any Jewish group saying that their executed leader had been raised from the dead, and he really was the Messiah after all.[16]

Ancient Judaism had no place for the resurrection of an isolated individual, especially of the Messiah. Therefore, after Jesus' crucifixion and burial, all the disciples could do was wait with longing for the general resurrection of the dead to be re-united their Master.

Left to their own devices, then, the disciples would not have come up with the idea that, contrary to Jewish beliefs, God had raised Jesus from the dead. This point undermines not only conspiracy theories, which imagine that the disciples *insincerely* proclaimed Jesus' resurrection, but also any theory which suggests that, on the basis of pagan or Jewish influences, they *sincerely* came to believe in and preached his resurrection.

> The Conspiracy Theory postulates motives and ideas and actions on the part of the earliest disciples for which we do not have a shred of evidence.

4. *Less contrived:* The Conspiracy Hypothesis—like all conspiracy theories of history—is contrived in supposing that what all the evidence seems to support is, in fact, mere appearance only, to be

explained away by hypotheses for which there is no evidence. Specifically, it postulates motives and ideas and actions on the part of the earliest disciples for which we do not have a shred of evidence. It can become quite elaborately contrived, as hypotheses are multiplied to ward off objections to the theory; for example, positing massive collusion to account for the appearance to the five hundred brethren, or inventing reasons to explain the unexpected role of women in the empty tomb and appearance stories.

5. *Disconfirmed by fewer accepted beliefs:* The Conspiracy Hypothesis is disconfirmed by our general knowledge of conspiracies, for they tend to be unstable and to unravel over time. Moreover, the hypothesis is disconfirmed by widely accepted beliefs about the disciples' sincerity, first century Jewish messianic expectations, and so on.

6. *Exceeds other hypotheses in fulfilling conditions 1–5:* Obviously this condition is not met, since there are hypotheses (such as the Hallucination Hypothesis), which don't dismiss the disciples' belief in Jesus' resurrection as a blatant lie and therefore do a better job of meeting the criteria.

No scholar defends the Conspiracy Hypothesis today. The only place you read about such notions is in the popular, sensationalist press or on the Internet.

APPARENT DEATH HYPOTHESIS

B iblical critics floated the Apparent Death Hypothesis early in the nineteenth century. They suggested that when Jesus was taken down from the cross, he wasn't really dead, but merely unconscious. He revived in the tomb and somehow escaped to convince his disciples he had risen from the dead. Once more, let's see how this hypothesis fares when assessed by our criteria for the best explanation:

> The Apparent Death Hypothesis suggests that when Jesus was taken down from the cross, he wasn't really dead, but merely unconscious.

1. *Explanatory scope*: The Apparent Death Hypothesis does provides explanations for the empty tomb, post-mortem appearances, and origin of the disciples' belief in Jesus' resurrection and so has adequate explanatory scope. That's a point in its favor.

2. *Explanatory power:* Here, the theory begins to break down. Some of the Apparent Death Hypotheses offered by critics were really versions of the old Conspiracy Hypothesis. Instead of stealing the body, the disciples (and sometimes Jesus himself!) were supposed

to be part of a conspiracy to fake Jesus' death on the cross. These versions of the theory therefore share all of the weaknesses of the Conspiracy Hypothesis.

> A non-conspiratorial version of the theory was that Jesus happened to survive the crucifixion by sheer luck.

A non-conspiratorial version of the theory was that Jesus happened to survive the crucifixion by sheer luck. This version of the hypothesis is also saddled with insurmountable problems; for example, how do you explain Jesus' empty tomb, since a man sealed inside couldn't move the massive stone lodged over the entrance? How do you explain Jesus' resurrection appearances, since a half-dead man desperately in need of medical attention would hardly have led the disciples to believe that he was the Risen Lord and conqueror of Death? How do you explain the origin of the disciples' belief in Jesus' resurrection, since their seeing him again would lead them only to conclude that he had managed to cheat death, not that he was, contrary to Jewish thought (as well as their own eyes), gloriously risen from the dead?

3. *Plausibility*: The Apparent Death Hypothesis is terribly implausible. Roman executioners could be relied upon to make sure that

> Roman executioners could be relied upon to make sure that their victims were dead!

their victims were dead! Since it's difficult to discern the precise moment of death by crucifixion, Roman executioners sometimes ensured death by a spear thrust into the victim's side. This is what happened Jesus' case (John 19:34). Moreover, the scenario that the hypothesis imagines is virtually impossible, medically speaking.

The Jewish historian Josephus tells how, when three men he knew were crucified, he managed to have them taken down from their crosses. Despite the best medical attention, two of the three died anyway.[17] The extent of Jesus' tortures was such that he could not plausibly have survived the crucifixion and entombment. And the idea that a man so critically wounded then went on to appear to the disciples on various occasions in both Jerusalem and Galilee is sheer fantasy.

4. *Less contrived*: The Apparent Death Hypothesis, especially in its conspiratorial versions, can become unbelievably contrived. We're supposed to imagine secret societies conspiring to fake Jesus' death, stealthily administered potions, conspiratorial alliances between Jesus' disciples and members of the Sanhedrin, and so forth, all with not a scrap of evidence in support.

> The Apparent Death Hypothesis has virtually no defenders among New Testament historians today.

5. *Disconfirmed by fewer accepted beliefs*: The Apparent Death Hypothesis is massively disconfirmed by what biology and modern medicine tell us about the pathology of a person who has been scourged and crucified. The unanimous evidence that Jesus did not continue to live among his disciples after his crucifixion also disconfirms it.

6. *Exceeds other hypotheses in fulfilling conditions 1–5:* The Apparent Death Hypothesis utterly fails this criterion. It has virtually no defenders among New Testament historians today.

CHAPTER THIRTEEN

DISPLACED BODY HYPOTHESIS

One of the few modern Jewish attempts to explain the facts concerning Jesus' fate was Joseph Klausner's proposal in 1922 that Joseph of Arimathea placed Jesus' body in his tomb only temporarily, because of the lateness of the hour and the proximity of his own family tomb to the place of Jesus' crucifixion. Klausner goes on to say that Joseph moved the corpse later to the common graveyard reserved for criminals. Unaware that Jesus' body had been displaced, the unwitting disciples, finding the tomb empty, inferred

> The Displaced Body Hypothesis suggests that Joseph of Arimathea placed Jesus' body in his tomb only temporarily, because of the lateness of the hour and the proximity of his own family tomb to the place of Jesus' crucifixion.

that Jesus was risen from the dead. Although no scholars defend Klausner's hypothesis today, I have seen attempts on the Internet to revive it. Its weaknesses are evident in light of what I have already said about the other theories:

1. *Explanatory scope:* The Displaced Body Hypothesis tries to explain the empty tomb, but says nothing about the post-mortem appearances and the origin of the disciples' belief in Jesus' resurrection. Independent hypotheses must be adopted to explain the full scope of the evidence.

2. *Explanatory power:* Obviously, Klausner's hypothesis has no explanatory power with regard to either the appearances or the origin of the Christian faith. What about the empty tomb? Here the hypothesis faces a rather obvious problem: Since Joseph, as well as any servants helping him, knew what they had done with the corpse, the theory is at a loss to explain why they didn't correct the disciples' blunder

> Jewish burial customs typically involved digging up the bones of the deceased after a year had passed and placing them in an ossuary.

once they began to proclaim that Jesus had been raised from the dead—unless, that is, one resorts to contrived conjectures to save the day, that Joseph and his servants suddenly died after moving the body!

Sometimes, people will object by saying that the disciples couldn't have been corrected, because Jesus' body would have decomposed beyond recognition. Therefore, it would have been futile for the Jewish authorities to point to the real location of Jesus' corpse; however, it's also not true. Jewish burial customs typically involved digging up the bones of the deceased after a year had passed and placing them in an ossuary. So gravesites, even for criminals, were carefully noted. And certainly, the body of a crucified man would have been identifiable from the injuries he sustained. In any case, the objection misses the central point: The earliest Jewish/ Christian disputes about Jesus' resurrection were not over the location of his grave or the identity of the corpse, but over why the tomb was empty. So, the alternative to the resurrection was theft. Had Joseph of Arimathea displaced the body, the Jewish/Christian controversy would have taken a very different course than the one it took.

3. *Plausibility:* The Displaced Body Hypothesis is implausible in a number of ways. In so far as we can rely on Jewish sources, the criminals' graveyard was located less than six hundred yards from the site of Jesus' crucifixion. Jewish regulations, moreover, required that executed criminals be interred immediately on the day of their execution. Therefore, Joseph both could and would have placed the body directly in the criminals' graveyard, thereby

> The earliest Jewish/ Christian disputes about Jesus' resurrection were not over the location of his grave or the identity of the corpse, but over why the tomb was empty.

> The criminals' graveyard was located less than six hundred yards from the site of Jesus' crucifixion. . . . Joseph both could and would have placed the body directly in the criminals' graveyard, thereby precluding any need to move it later or defile his own family tomb with the corpse of a criminal.

precluding any need to move it later or defile his own family tomb with the corpse of a criminal. In fact, Jewish law actually forbade moving a body later, unless it was to the family tomb of the deceased. Joseph had adequate time prior to sunset for a simple burial, which probably included washing the corpse and wrapping it up in a sheet with dry spices.

4. *Less contrived:* The theory is a bit contrived in ascribing to Joseph motives and activities for which we have no evidence at all. It becomes very contrived if we have to start inventing things like Joseph's death in order to save the hypothesis.

5. *Disconfirmed by fewer accepted beliefs:* The Displaced Body Hypothesis is disconfirmed by what we know about the Jewish burial procedures for criminals, which were mentioned in the third point.

6. *Exceeds other hypotheses in fulfilling conditions 1–5:* Again, no historian shares this estimation of the theory's worth.

CHAPTER FOURTEEN

HALLUCINATION HYPOTHESIS

Back in 1835, in his book *The Life of Jesus, Critically Examined*, the German biblical critic David Friedrich Strauss proposed that the resurrection appearances were merely hallucinations on the disciples' part. The most prominent defender of the Hallucination Hypothesis today is the German New Testament critic Gerd Lüdemann. How does it fare when assessed by our criteria?

1. *Explanatory scope:* The Hallucination Hypothesis has inadequate explanatory scope. First, it says nothing to explain the empty tomb. Therefore, one must either deny the fact of the empty tomb (and, therefore, the burial as well) or else conjoin an independent hypothesis to the Hallucination Hypothesis to account for the empty tomb.

> The Hallucination Hypothesis fails to explain the origin of the disciples' belief in Jesus' resurrection.

Second, the Hallucination Hypothesis fails to explain the origin of the disciples' belief in Jesus' resurrection. Some scholars have made a great deal out of the alleged similarities between the post-mortem appearances of Jesus and visions of recently departed loved ones on the part of bereaved persons. But while such visions are certainly intriguing, the overriding lesson of such experiences is that the bereaved do not as a result of such visions—however real and tangible they may seem—conclude that their deceased loved one has come physically back to life. Rather, the bereaved believe that they have seen their deceased loved one in the afterlife. As N. T. Wright observes, for someone in the ancient world, visions of the deceased were not taken as evidence that the person is alive, but as evidence that he is dead!

> For someone in the ancient world, visions of the deceased were not taken as evidence that the person is alive, but as evidence that he is dead!

Moreover, in a Jewish context there are more appropriate interpretations of such experiences besides resurrection. Were the disciples to project visions of Jesus after his death, then—given Jewish beliefs about life after death—they would have seen Jesus in heaven or in Abraham's bosom, where Jews believed the souls of the righteous dead went to abide until the final resurrection. Such visions would not have led, however, to belief in Jesus' resurrection; at the most, it would have only led the disciples to say that Jesus had been assumed into heaven, not raised from the dead.

> In Jewish thinking, an assumption into heaven is not the same as a resurrection.

In Jewish thinking, an assumption into heaven is not the same as a resurrection. Assumption is God's taking someone bodily out of this world into heaven; for example, in the Old Testament stories of Enoch and Elijah, these men did not die but were taken directly into heaven by God. A dead person might also be assumed into heaven. In an extra-biblical Jewish writing called The Testament of Job (40), the story is told of two children killed in the collapse of a house. When the rescuers clear away the rubble, the bodies of the children are nowhere to be found. Meanwhile, their mother sees a vision of the two children glorified in heaven, where God has taken them up.

In contrast to assumption into heaven, the Jewish conception of resurrection is God's raising up of a dead person in the space-time universe. The person is not taken out of this world, but raised up in it. Assumption and resurrection are, therefore, distinct categories in Jewish thought.

Given Jewish beliefs concerning assumption and resurrection, the discovery of the empty tomb and hallucinations of Jesus would at most have caused the disciples to think that Jesus had been assumed into glory, for this was consistent with their Jewish frame of thought. But they wouldn't have come to believe that Jesus had been raised from the dead, for this fundamentally contradicted Jewish beliefs about the resurrection of the dead. Thus, even given hallucinations, belief in Jesus' resurrection remains unexplained.

2. *Explanatory power*: Not only does the Hallucination Hypothesis say nothing to explain the empty tomb and the origin of the disciples' belief in Jesus' resurrection, but it also has weak explanatory power even when it comes to explaining the appearances. Let's suppose that Peter experienced a guilt-induced vision of Jesus, as Lüdemann imagines, or, more plausibly, was one of those people who experience a vision of a deceased loved one. Would this supposition suffice to explain the resurrection appearances? Not really, for the diversity of the appearances bursts the bounds of anything found in the psychological casebooks. Think about it: Jesus appeared not just one time, but many times; not at just one locale and under one circumstance, but at a variety of places and

under a variety of circumstances; not to just one individual, but to different persons; not just to individuals, but to various groups; not just to believers, but to unbelievers . . . and even enemies. Positing a chain reaction among the disciples won't solve the problem, because people like James and Paul don't stand in the chain; so those who would explain the resurrection appearances psychologically have to construct a composite picture by cobbling together different, unrelated cases of hallucinatory experiences. The necessity of this expedient only serves to underline the fact that there's nothing like the resurrection appearances in the psychological casebooks.

3. *Plausibility*: Lüdemann attempts to make his Hallucination Hypothesis plausible by means of psychoanalyses of Peter and Paul. He believes that they both labored under guilt complexes, which found release in the hallucinations of Jesus. But Lüdemann's psychoanalysis is implausible for at least three reasons: First, Lüdemann's use of depth psychology is based upon certain theories of Jung and Freud, which are widely rejected. Second, there's not enough information to do psychoanalyses of Peter or Paul. Psychoanalysis is difficult enough to carry out even with patients on the psychoanalyst's couch, so to speak, but it's next to impossible with historical figures. That's why historians reject the genre of psychobiography today. Finally, third, the evidence we do have suggests that Paul did not struggle with a guilt complex as Lüdemann supposes.

> Psychoanalysis is difficult enough to carry out even with patients on the psychoanalyst's couch, so to speak, but it's next to impossible with historical figures.

IMPLAUSIBILITY OF LÜDEMANN'S PSYCHOANALYSIS
OF PETER AND PAUL

Depth psychology is based upon certain theories of Jung and Freud, which are widely rejected

Lack of information to perform psychoanalysis, because Peter and Paul are historical figures (that's why the genre of psycho-biography is rejected by historians today)

Evidence available suggests that Paul did not struggle with a guilt complex, as Lüdemann supposes

....

Nearly fifty years ago, the Swedish scholar Krister Stendahl pointed out that Western readers have tended to read Paul through the lenses of Martin Luther's struggles with guilt and sin. But Paul (or Saul) the Pharisee experienced no such struggle. Stendahl writes:

> *Contrast Paul, a very happy and successful Jew, one who can say 'As to righteousness under the Law (I was) blameless' (Phil. 3.6). That is what he says. He experiences no troubles, no problems, and no qualms of conscience. He is a star pupil, the student to get the thousand dollar graduate scholarship in Gamaliel's Seminary. . . . Nowhere in Paul's writings is there any indication . . . that psychologically Paul had some problem of conscience.[18]*

In order to justify his portrait of a guilt-ridden Paul, Lüdemann is compelled to interpret Romans 7 as a description of Paul's pre-Christian experience. But since the late 1920s, almost all commentators have rejected this autobiographical interpretation of Romans 7, so Lüdemann's psychoanalysis is positively implausible.

A second way in which the Hallucination Hypothesis is implausible is by its designating the appearances to be merely visionary experiences. Lüdemann recognizes that the Hallucination Hypothesis stands or falls on the assumption that what Paul experienced on the Damascus Road was the same as what all the other disciples experienced; but this assumption is groundless. In including himself in the list of eyewitnesses to Christ's resurrection appearances, Paul in no way implies that the other appearances were just like the appearance he saw. Many of Paul's opponents in Corinth denied that he was a true apostle, so Paul is anxious to include himself along with the other apostles who had seen Christ. Paul is trying to bring his experience on the Damascus Road up to the objectivity and reality of theirs, not to pull their experience down to merely visionary experiences.

So the Hallucination Hypothesis is implausible both with regard to its psychoanalysis of the witnesses and with regard to its blanket reduction of the appearances to visionary experiences.

4. *Less contrived:* Lüdemann's version of the Hallucination Hypothesis is contrived in a number of ways; for example, he assumes that the disciples fled back to Galilee after Jesus' arrest; that Peter was so obsessed with guilt that he projected a hallucination of Jesus; that the other disciples were also prone to hallucinations; and that Paul had a struggle with the Jewish law, and a secret attraction to Christianity. There is no evidence for any of these assumptions.

5. *Disconfirmed by fewer accepted beliefs:* Some of the accepted beliefs of New Testament scholars today tend to disconfirm the Hallucination Hypothesis, at least in the way that Lüdemann presents it. Examples include: the belief that Jesus was laid in a tomb by Joseph of Arimathea; that Jesus' tomb was discovered empty by women; that psychoanalysis of historical figures is not feasible; that Paul was basically content with his life under the Jewish law; and that the New Testament makes a distinction between a mere vision and a resurrection appearance.

6. *Exceeds other hypotheses in fulfilling conditions 1–5:* The Hallucination Hypothesis remains a live option today and in that respect, has outstripped its rivals. But the crucial question is whether it outstrips the Resurrection Hypothesis.

CHAPTER FIFTEEN

THE RESURRECTION HYPOTHESIS

W e've seen how poorly the customary explanations of the empty tomb, the post-mortem appearances, and the origin of the disciples' faith fare when assessed by standard criteria for testing historical hypotheses. They're especially weak when it comes to explanatory scope and power and are often highly implausible.

> The Resurrection Hypothesis has greater explanatory scope than certain other explanations like the Hallucination Hypothesis or the Displaced Body Hypothesis precisely because it can explain all three of the main facts at issue.

But does the Resurrection Hypothesis do any better as an explanation of the evidence? Is it a better explanation than the implausible naturalistic explanations offered in the past? In order to answer these questions, let's apply the same criteria to the hypothesis that "God raised Jesus from the dead."

1. *Explanatory scope:* The Resurrection Hypothesis has greater explanatory scope than certain other explanations like the Hallucination Hypothesis or the Displaced Body Hypothesis precisely be-

cause it can explain all three of the main facts at issue—whereas, the rival hypotheses try to explain only one.

2. *Explanatory power:* This is, I think, the greatest virtue of the Resurrection Hypothesis. The Conspiracy Hypothesis and the Apparent Death Hypothesis, by contrast, just do not convincingly account for the empty tomb, resurrection appearances, or origin of the Christian faith; on these theories, the evidence (such as the transformation of the disciples) becomes very improbable. By contrast, on the hypothesis of Jesus' resurrection, it seems extremely probable that the tomb should be empty, that the disciples should see appearances of Jesus alive, and that they should come to believe in his resurrection.

3. *Plausibility:* The plausibility of Jesus' resurrection grows exponentially once we consider it in its proper philosophical context: namely, a theistic worldview, in its historical context, and Jesus' own unparalleled life/radical personal claims. Given that God exists, the hypothesis that God would raise Jesus of Nazareth from the dead cannot be said to be implausible.

> The plausibility of Jesus' resurrection grows exponentially once we consider it in its proper philosophical context: namely, a theistic worldview, in its historical context, and Jesus' own unparalleled life/radical personal claims.

4. *Less contrived:* The Resurrection Hypothesis possesses great explanatory scope and power, but some scholars have charged that it is contrived. Being contrived, if you recall, is a matter of how many new suppositions a hypothesis must make which are not implied by existing knowledge.

> It's hard to see why the Resurrection Hypothesis is extraordinarily contrived. It requires only one new supposition: that God exists.

By definition, however, it's hard to see why the Resurrection Hypothesis is extraordinarily contrived. It requires only one new supposition: that God exists. Surely its rival hypotheses require many more new suppositions. For example, the Conspiracy Hypothesis requires us to suppose that the moral character of the disciples was defective, which is certainly not implied by already existing knowledge; the Apparent Death Hypothesis requires the supposition that the centurion's spear thrust into Jesus' side was just a superficial poke or is an unhistorical detail in the narrative, which again goes beyond existing knowledge; the Hallucination Hypothesis requires us to suppose some sort of emotional preparation of the disciples, which predisposed them to project visions of Jesus alive—again, not implied by our knowledge. And there are many more examples that could be listed—the aforementioned are just a few.

It should be noted, too, that scientific hypotheses regularly include the supposition of the existence of new entities, such as quarks, strings, gravitons, black holes, and the like, without those theories being characterized as contrived. Moreover, for the person who already believes in God, the Resurrection Hypothesis doesn't even introduce the new supposition of God's existence, since that's already implied by his existing knowledge. So the Resurrection Hypothesis cannot be said to be contrived simply by virtue of the number of new suppositions it introduces.

If our hypothesis is contrived, then, it must be for some other reasons. Philosophers of science have found it notoriously difficult to explain what it is exactly that makes a hypothesis contrived. There seems to be an air of artificiality about a hypothesis charged as contrived, which can be sensed by those who are seasoned practitioners of the relevant science.

Now I think that the sense of discomfort that many people, even Christians, feel about appealing to God as part of an explanatory hypothesis for some phenomenon in the world is that doing so has this air of artificiality about it—just seems too easy when confronted with some unexplained phenomenon to throw up one's hands and say, "God did it!" Is the hypothesis that "God raised Jesus from the dead" contrived, in this sense?

I don't think so. A supernatural explanation of the empty tomb, the resurrection appearances, and the origin of the Christian faith is not contrived given the context of Jesus' own unparalleled life, ministry, and personal claims. A supernatural hypothesis is appropriate in such a context. It's also precisely because of this historical context that the Resurrection Hypothesis does not seem contrived when compared to miraculous explanations of other sorts; for example, that a "psychological miracle" occurred, causing normal men and women to become conspirators and liars who would be martyred willingly for their lies; or that a "biological miracle" occurred, which prevented Jesus' dying on the cross (despite the spear-thrust through his chest, and so forth). It is these miraculous hypotheses that strike us as artificial and contrived, not the Resurrection Hypothesis, which makes abundantly good sense in the context of Jesus' ministry and radical personal claims. Thus, it seems to me that the Resurrection Hypothesis cannot be characterized as excessively contrived.

5. *Disconfirmed by fewer accepted beliefs:* I can't think of any accepted beliefs which disconfirm the Resurrection Hypothesis— unless one thinks that, say, "Dead men do not rise" disconfirms the

hypothesis. But this generalization does nothing to disconfirm our hypothesis that God raised Jesus from the dead. We may consistently believe both—that men do not rise naturally from the dead and that God raised Jesus from the dead. By contrast, rival theories are disconfirmed by accepted beliefs about, for example, the instability of conspiracies, the likelihood of death as a result of crucifixion, the psychological characteristics of hallucinatory experiences, and so forth, as we have seen.

> We may consistently believe that men do not rise naturally from the dead and that God raised Jesus from the dead.

6. *Exceeds other hypotheses in fulfilling conditions 1–5:* There's certainly little chance that any of the rival hypotheses will ever exceed the Resurrection Hypothesis in fulfilling the above conditions. When confronted with the facts of the empty tomb, the resurrection appearances, and the origin of the Christian faith, the stupefaction of contemporary scholarship suggests that no better rival is anywhere on the horizon. Once you give up the prejudice against miracles, it's hard to deny that the resurrection of Jesus is the best explanation of the facts.

CONCLUSION

In conclusion, therefore, three great, independently established facts—the empty tomb, the resurrection appearances, and the origin of the Christian faith—all point to the same marvelous conclusion: that God raised Jesus from the dead. Given that God exists, this conclusion cannot be barred to anyone seeking for the truth about Jesus.

ENDNOTES

1 Craig, William L., "Does God Exist? Responding to the New Atheism" (working paper, Impact 360 Institute, Atlanta, 2014).

2 Horst Georg Pöhlmann, *Abriss der Dogmatik*, 3rd rev. ed. (Düsseldorf: Patmos Verlag, 1966), 230.

3 John A. T. Robinson, *The Human Face of God* (Philadelphia: Westminster, 1973), 131.

4 *Antiquities,* IV.8.15

5 Sotah, 19a.

6 Kiddushin, 82b.

7 Berachos, 60b.

8 Jacob Kremer, *Die Osterevangelien—Geschichten um Geschichte* (Stuttgart: Katholisches Bibelwerk, 1977), 49–50.

9 Gary Habermas, "Experience of the Risen Jesus: The Foundational Historical Issue in the Early Proclamation of the Resurrection," *Dialog* 45 (2006): 292.

10 C. H. Dodd, "The Appearances of the Risen Christ: A study in the form criticism of the Gospels," in *More New Testament Studies* (Manchester: University of Manchester, 1968), 128.

11 *Antiquities,* 20.200.

12 Hans Grass, *Ostergeschehen und Osterberichte*, 4th ed. (Göttingen: Vandenhoeck & Ruprecht, 1974), 80.

13 Gerd Lüdemann, *What Really Happened to Jesus?*, trans. John Bowden (Louisville, Kent.: Westminster John Knox Press, 1995), 80.

14 R. H. Fuller, *The Formation of the Resurrection Narratives* (London: SPCK, 1972), 2.

15 C. Behan McCullagh, *Justifying Historical Descriptions* (Cambridge: Cambridge University Press, 1984), 19.

16 N. T. Wright, lecture at Asbury College and Seminary, 1999.

17 The *Life of Flavius Josephus* 75. 420–1.

18 Krister Stendahl, "Paul among Jews and Gentiles," in *Paul among Jews and Gentiles* (Philadelphia: Fortess Press, 1976), 12–13.

About William Lane Craig, Ph.D.

William Lane Craig is Research Professor of Philosophy at Talbot School of Theology in La Mirada, California. He and his wife Jan have two grown children.

At the age of sixteen as a junior in high school, he first heard the message of the Christian gospel and yielded his life to Christ. Dr. Craig pursued his undergraduate studies at Wheaton College (B.A. 1971) and graduate studies at Trinity Evangelical Divinity School (M.A. 1974; M.A. 1975), the University of Birmingham (England) (Ph.D. 1977), and the University of Munich (Germany) (D.Theol. 1984). From 1980-86 he taught Philosophy of Religion at Trinity, during which time he and Jan started their family. In 1987 they moved to Brussels, Belgium, where Dr. Craig pursued research at the University of Louvain until assuming his position at Talbot in 1994.

He has authored or edited over thirty books, including *The Kalam Cosmological Argument*; *Assessing the New Testament Evidence for the Historicity of the Resurrection of Jesus*; *Divine Foreknowledge and Human Freedom*; *Theism, Atheism and Big Bang Cosmology*; and *God, Time and Eternity*, as well as over a hundred articles in professional journals of philosophy and theology, including *The Journal of Philosophy, New Testament Studies, Journal for the Study of the New Testament, American Philosophical Quarterly, Philosophical Studies, Philosophy*, and *British Journal for Philosophy of Science*.

Find out more: reasonablefaith.org